100
THINGS
→TO←
WRITE
ABOUT

RON KOERTGE
PASADENA CITY COLLEGE

 LONGMAN

100 THINGS TO WRITE ABOUT

ISBN: 0-673-98239-4

98 99 00 9 8 7 6 5

Table of Contents

Introduction   v

Assignments by Rhetorical Type   ix

Assignments by Theme   xi

100 Things to Write About: Assignments 1-100   1

Introduction

A lot of what this book is about can be found on the next couple of pages. Read through them before you do any of the exercises. All of the important points will be repeated, but start here. Pretend that you have to write a paragraph. Here's the assignment:

Would you rather own a station wagon, a four-wheel-drive vehicle, or a sports car?

First of all the Topic is something general like Cars. The assignment asks you to prefer one kind over another and to write a paragraph about it. So you need a starting point, something to work from that will help you write a sensible paragraph. By itself, the topic — Cars — is too fat to handle. What you need is a Thesis Sentence.

A Thesis is simply a one-sentence statement (usually the first sentence in the paragraph or essay) that commits you to something you can finish writing about in a short time. For example, "I prefer station wagons because they're better" may not work. *Better* is a vague word; it can mean lots of things. But "I prefer station wagons because I have six kids" nails it right down.

To get a feel for the differences among Topics, Weak Thesis and Strong Thesis, take a look at these:

Topic Running
Weak Thesis   Running is good for people.
Stronger Thesis Running has already helped me look and feel younger.

Topic Reading
Weak Thesis   Reading can pass the time pleasantly for most of us.
Stronger Thesis   Reading science-fiction gets me away from my problems and helps me relax.
So much for Topics and the Thesis for a minute. Now let's talk about Development which means the same thing as building or explaining. Every Thesis has some key words in it. In "I prefer station wagons because they're better" the most important key word is *better*. But the natural question is this: better in what ways? Are they faster, bigger, more efficient or what? If all those questions are answered, how long did this little assignment get all of a sudden? Too long, I'm afraid.

But "prefer station wagons because I have six kids" might develop like this:

I prefer station wagons because I have six kids. A car, even a four-door one, is just too small for me. By the time I get the twins in the wagon plus their strollers and about a hundred Pampers, I've already used most of the space I'd find in a Toyota or a mid-sized Dodge.

This little paragraph develops from its key words (six kids) and it does it very naturally, telling exactly why wagons are more useful than other kinds of cars. The man or woman who wrote it sounds real. And, even though some of the details may have been changed to make a good paragraph, it sounds true or at least true-to-life.

Keep these things in mind as you work through this book:

1.   Get yourself a Thesis that is likely to develop into just the length of paragraph or essay you've been assigned.

2.   Pay attention to the key words, the ones that need expanding or explaining.

3.   Use real examples from the real world.

Assignments by Rhetorical Type

Exposition: 1, 2, 9, 10, 11, 20, 24, 41, 46, 50, 51, 53, 56, 60, 63, 64, 72, 79, 80, 82, 87, 94, 97, 99, 100

Argumentation: 5, 6, 12, 14, 21, 25, 27, 35, 38, 45, 47, 48, 54, 68, 69, 71, 73, 75, 84, 89, 92, 93

Description: 22, 23, 28, 36, 39, 44, 55, 57, 90

Definition: 8, 15, 17, 18, 19, 26, 32, 33, 52, 66, 67, 95, 96, 98

Cause & Effect: 3, 29, 37, 40,42, , 65, 70, 76, 77, 78, 85, 88, 91

Comparison/Contrast: 16, 30, 31, 34, 49, 58, 59, 62, 74, 81

Process: 4, 7, 13, 86

Classification: 43, 61, 83

Assignments by Theme

Values & Evaluations: 5, 6, 9, 23, 32, 36,39, 47, 53, 57, 63, 7075, 79, 80, 87, 91, 94, 95.

Self-Knowledge: 1, 7, 8, 18, 20, 22,29 ,30, 46, 50, 64, 65, 74, 78, 85, 86, 100

American Culture: 2, 4, 15, 21, 33, 34, 35, 43, 54, 60, 67, 71,89, 93, 96, 99.

Human Behavior: 3, 19, 31, 42, 49, 66, 68, 72, 76, 81, 83,90, 92, 98

Gender Issues: 17, 37, 44, 52, 62, 69, 73,

Relations With Others: 10, 11, 27, 41, 55, 56, 58, 59, 97

Media: 12, 14, 24, 25, 28, 38, 51, 77

Education: 13, 16, 26, 40, 45, 48, 61, 82, 84, 88

Assignment 1

Do you think you're a well-organized person? Write a paragraph explaining why you feel you are or aren't.

Comment: I think the simplest way to solve this writing problem — and that's what they all are — is to start the thesis with a Yes or No; then tack the word *because* on, and finish by answering the question:

Yes, I think I'm well-organized since I never misplace anything.

Or:

No, I don't think I'm well-organized because my room is a mess.

Look for the key words, and develop those. Show the mess. Don't just say that things are all over the place. Say that your sweaters are on the closet floor and your goldfish is somewhere among among your socks. Now that's a mess.

By the way, sometimes your teacher won't want you to use my sample thesis sentences I give. Just remember that most of the time you can just unplug my key words and plug in your own after the *because*. That's not cheating.

Assignment 2

Identify one of the ways Americans are wasteful. Write a paragraph only.

Comment: Don't be afraid to try out a few different thesis sentences on scratch paper. This is not too demanding an assignment since it asks for only "one of the ways," so a thesis with a single key word will do. Don't try "Americans waste salad dressing and motor oil." That has one key word to many

Whether you feel that Americans waste their food, their energy, their gasoline, or their time, remember to develop the whole essay. A skimpy paragraph is something like a page in a coloring book. Only the outlines are there. So fill everything in.

Americans waste water. Last night I counted five dripping faucets in my house, and one of them sounded like it was right next to the bed. When I came home late last week, half the sprinklers in the neighborhood were on, and it was raining. Finally, when I went downstairs to do a load of laundry, the machine was churning away with one pair of my stupid sister's socks in it.

Assignment 3

Lots of people are wearing T-shirts and jackets with writing on them. Sometimes they do the writing themselves; usually they buy the shirts already printed or have their own messages ironed on. What do you think is the main reason that people wear clothes like these?

Comment: Here you're asked for one reason, the main one, so a few minutes jotting down possibilities might help. Once you're finished, consider this: the main reason for anything is always arguable, so don't worry about getting the perfect reason. Do look for the obvious ones (to be stylish, to get attention, to irritate people, to show off), and stay away from the merely strange (to keep warm, to cover tattoos).

You absolutely have to give examples of the clothes that you've seen. Otherwise, how will the person who's reading your paragraph know exactly what you're talking about? Also, let's face it, Bob probably wears a BAN THE BOMB T-shirt for a different reason than Sue's I LOVE ROMEO PEAK.
Let me give you a look at just part of a paragraph that needs more real examples:

The writing on people's shirts and jackets always says something different or it might make people laugh and that gets attention.

What does *different* mean? What exactly did it say that was funny?

Assignment 4

If you could make up a new holiday, what would it be? When would it be? How would the nation celebrate?

Comment: Notice that the What and When of this assignment can probably be answered quickly, and the real key word — the one that takes the most development — is *How*.
Here are two possible beginnings for this one:

I would have Bobby Day, a holiday named after myself. It'd be June l, right after school is out and everybody named Bobby or knew a Bobby or wanted to be named Bobby could come to my house and swim.

I'd like to invent Wicked Stepmother Day. I'd hold it at noon in Tucson, Arizona, in August. Everybody would send their wicked stepmothers and I'd arrange to have them bussed out to the desert for a huge, steaming dinner. Then the busses would pull away and leave them there.

Start with a thesis. If you come up with something blah ("I'd have Fun Day on June 1, and everybody would celebrate by having fun") and you just can't get anything else, do what you can with it. If you could go on and be specific about the kind of fun people might have, if you'd give real examples that actually sound like fun, you might be able to pull it off.

Assignment 5

Some people say they like to get outdoors — to the desert or beach or mountains — because they can't feel a connection to anything valuable in the city. Do you think it's true that in the city we're more or less disconnected from qualities that really exist somewhere outside the city limits?

Comment: Though there are other good ways, this thesis might simply begin with a "Yes, I do think we're disconnected . . . " Or a "No, I don't think we're disconnected . . . " But I'll bet the key to tackling this assignment successfully is to make clear what the word *qualities* means. Here's a guy who's spent too much time alone in the woods:

In the city I can't feel the universal forces that are in the country, those forces that make us all human and not just slaves of the machine. I live for those moments away from my desk when the goodness of the universe pours through me via the grass and trees.

As you jot down possible valuable qualities that people might be able to connect to outside the city (maybe just how pretty things are or how quiet), don't be afraid to flip-flop your thesis. If you don't find examples to support a Yes-thesis, just try one beginning with a No:

No, I don't think there are any special qualities outside the city. I can find peace and quiet in Lacey Park. Lying on the grass there is just as restful as at Ghost Lips Lake. I'm probably more connected to serenity in the city because I'm not half crazy from making the drive up to the lake!

Assignment 6

The circus came to town last week, and a handful of protesters outside picketed as advocates-of-the-animals. Do you feel that circuses are cruel, unnatural, and exploitative? Or are they fun and are the animals lucky to have such good care and attention?

Comment: People argue in bars, couples argue, schools have debate teams and teachers assign Argumentative papers. This assignment asks you to pick just one side of the circus-controversy.

Trying to convince someone to see your side of things is different from merely telling him or her how you feel about hiking. Some arguments can get pretty hot. That's okay here, too. Remember: if you claim that circuses are fun, show how much fun they are. Don't just say so, hoping that your readers will fill in with circus memories of their own. Here are two different openings to mull over:

I can't imagine a circus without elephants lumbering around, standing on their hind legs and picking up pretty girls with their trunks. I guess it's selfish to want to see this and to never think about how the animal feels, but I can't help it. The circus wouldn't be the circus without animals.

I admit that circus animals aren't in danger of being killed and eaten by predators, but this safety is at the expense of their freedom. That's not a choice many humans would make, so I can't help but feel that the animals are being exploited.

Assignment 7

A recent survey by *Time* magazine shows that as many as seven out of ten people are unhappy with their jobs. What can you do now to help insure that you won't be an unhappy and frustrated employee?

Comment: First, concentrate on the most important sentence in this assignment: "What can you do now . . .?" You can write a fine thesis by just repeating some of the key words from that sentence: For example, "So that I won't be unhappy and frustrated when I'm thirty-five, right now I'm staying in school. I don't want to end up working on the dock at Slo-Mo Inc. for the rest of my life."

Here are some more openings to consider and to remind you that writing isn't like math. There's more than one way to solve these problems. You may not agree with these thesis sentences; they may seem naive or idealistic or downright goofy. But as long as the writers develop them specifically and clearly, they're on their way to decent papers.

I know I can't afford to marry my boyfriend and have a family if I really want to be a good real estate salesperson, so right now I'm putting marriage off rather than settle for a job that'll make me unhappy.

I'm nineteen and I plan to get married next year because I know a stable family life will motivate me to work hard and to be happy.

Right now I'm carefully planning every college course I take so I won't waste any time and I'll get my degree in Engineering fast.

Assignment 8

What do you think it means to be mature?

Comment: First of all, make sure you know how long this paper is supposed to be. If your teacher didn't announce it, ask. You know now that "I think a mature person doesn't get mad as easily as an immature one" will introduce a different-sized paragraph than "Maturity doesn't have much to do with anything except age." Neither is wrong or right so much as each is different.

To be mature is to act grown-up in all ways, especially when it really counts. This means letting go of childhood habits and forcing yourself, if necessary, to do the mature thing.

This opening isn't promising enough for most writing teachers. It just tosses the words *mature* and *grown-up* around as if we all knew exactly what they meant. Try this:

I learned what it meant to be mature when I was fifteen and my folks split up. All of a sudden I had to balance the checking account, pay the bills, do laundry for four people, and clip food coupons out of the newspaper.

See the difference?

Assignment 9

"It doesn't take any more time to do it right." In your experience, is this true?

Comment: This kind of assignment, the in-your-experience assignment, is worth looking at because it comes up so often. It points out the difference between writing and math. 2 + 2 is always 4, but if you and your friend go to Disneyland, you might like it and she might hate it. Same experience; different conclusion._Now, down to business. First, the test here is not to bury your teacher in information or philosophy, but to build a sensible-sounding paragraph. The easy thesis is this: "In my experience, it does/does not take any more time to do it right." Now follow that immediately with examples. Talk about cooking, studying, hanging wallpaper, fixing an engine, sewing, or being a hit man for the Mafia.

Here's a paragraph that isn't finished, but it does begin to do what I suggested — a thesis followed immediately by the first example:

In my experience, it doesn't take any more time to do it right. When I worked at McDonald's and we cleaned the grill or mopped the floor in a hurry, we always had to just do it over.

To finish up, let me show you a thesis that's a little different, but just as good:

When I'm cooking and I try to cut corners, I usually end up regretting it.

If this is followed by a description of cakes as tall as pizzas or holiday meals that ended in bloodshed, the paragraph should be fine.

Assignment 10

What can you figure out about someone merely by knowing who his enemies are?

Comment: First, a reminder. Nearly all teachers like to see most of the assignment in the thesis, so instead of just answering the question ("I might learn that he is obnoxious."), use some of the key words: "By knowing someone's enemies, I might be able to figure out that he's obnoxious or — if his enemies are creeps — that he's an okay guy."

This is an assignment to be read very carefully. It does *not* say, "What can you learn about a person who has enemies?" It asks what you can learn about him by knowing *who* his enemies are. So the basic idea of the thesis is this: "I might learn that someone is _____ by knowing who his enemies are." Depending on how long the assignment is, the blank can be filled in by one word or more than one: trustworthy, dishonest, a creep, an okay guy, to be avoided, etc.

I think students can learn as much about composition by seeing bad writing as they can by seeing good. Here's an awful opening, wordy and vague, followed by a revised version:

I could learn that someone is a bad person if good people dislike him or her. If he or she is so unpopular, he or she must have done something bad.

I trust my friends, so if they don't like someone, there's a good chance he's a trouble-maker. This turned out to be true with Bob.

Assignment 11

All our lives we listen to people: fathers, mothers, brothers and sisters, teachers, religious leaders, and so forth. They give advice about how to live, think, and behave. How do you know when it's time to stop listening to others?

Comment: Let me start by showing you how *not* to write this essay (or any other).

It's time to stop listening to others when they don't give good advice. Everyone tells us what to do, but not everyone is right. Sometimes they're wrong, and they're so wrong somebody could get hurt. Even parents who mean well can be wrong, so when they are, that's the time to stop listening.

What you've just read probably has its heart in the right place, and there's certainly some truth in it, but it can't be rewarded in school because it isn't organized and it isn't clear. Whom are we reading about ? What does *wrong* mean? What advice did Dad give about going to school that was so bad?
Finally, I didn't give some of my usual sample thesis sentences, so fool around with some possibilities on scratch paper. Just read the last sentence of the assignment once or twice. Use some of the key words in your thesis. Then add your examples. If one long one will do, that's fine. If two or three shorter ones are more appropriate, that's fine, too.

Assignment 12

Do you think advertisements appeal more to needs than to wants or more to wants than needs?

Comment: This is the standard either/or assignment, so you'll simply have to commit yourself and think of examples that will make sense.

I have three pieces of advice. What sort of advertisements do you want to use? It might be okay to lump billboards, radio, and TV together, but consider limiting yourself to one kind of advertisement. A thesis like this — "Ads on radio tend to be straightforward and informative, so they appeal mostly to needs rather than wants." — has a real focus to it, something a reader can concentrate on. Writing about all ads everywhere feels mushy. Pick one kind of advertisement and stick to it.

Second, be specific about the differences between needs and wants. More often than not the key words in an assignment or a thesis will need some explaining. After all, one man's need ("I need a massage because I work so hard I can't sleep otherwise.") is another's want ("Sure, I want a massage, but I can sleep without one."). You're the writer here; what do the words mean to you?

Finally, you should use the names of real products. *Coke* is real; *soft drink* is vague. *Volkswagen* is real; *car* is vague. *A trip to Hawaii on Delta Airlines* is real; *a vacation by plane* is vague.

Assignment 13

How would you begin to teach a young child the difference between good people and bad ones?

Comment: First, try to sense the real intention here. One thing we've been working with in the first part of this book is just reading the assignment clearly and seeing exactly what's needed. Give yourself a little test. Look back at the assignment and pick out the key words. Which one tells you that this assignment can probably be done in a paragraph or very short essay? If you picked *begin,* you're right. You're asked only how you'd begin to do this, so something short will do, and it can still be complete and sensible. Here are some examples of useful thesis sentences :

I'd use TV shows to begin teaching kids the difference between good people and bad.

I'd begin to teach my child the difference between good people and bad ones by reading him stories from the Bible.

Fairy tales, with their obvious villains and heroes, would be good for children just starting to learn who's good and bad.

Whenever you're stuck or confused, remember your own life and experiences. Think back to how you were taught. Would you begin to teach other young children like that?

Assignment 14

A recent FCC (Federal Communications Commission) tackled the issue of what a person can say or sing over the radio. One side claims that laying down strict guidelines eventually leads to the end of every kind of freedom. The other argues that since any child can turn the radio on at any time, there have to be rules and regulations. Do your experiences suggest limiting what can be broadcast?

Comment: The part of this assignment that I like is the sentence beginning, "Do your experiences suggest . . .?" You're not asked to know everything about the issue; you're not asked to do research on censorship, freedom of speech, or the corruption of today's youth. What do your experiences suggest? Here are two possibilities:

I think there should be limits on what kids can hear on the radio. When I was nine, I caught part of a Lenny Bruce album on some obscure FM station. He used all the four-letter words and told crude jokes. It all made me a little queasy and upset. Now I wouldn't think much about it, but back then I really wasn't ready.

I've never heard anything on the radio that I haven't heard at school or seen written on a wall. Nobody I know is shocked by songs about love, and I wouldn't want to start something that would end up censoring almost everything.

What do your experiences suggest?

Assignment 15

In a recent TV commercial, a well-known actor begins his pitch like this: "I like the good life." Then he goes on to describe beaches, palm trees, and his favorite airline. Write a long paragraph or short essay about your idea of the good life.

Comment: For most students this will fall into the category of Descriptive writing where they're not asked to explain (Exposition) or convince (Argumentation) but to let a reader see, smell, feel, touch and/or hear the things that make up "the good life." Many beginning writers think that Description is just, "The grass is green. The sky is blue." But that's only *telling*. I'm talking about *showing*.

The assigned length makes this a little tough. Don't insist on cramming the entire good life into a paragraph if it won't fit. "My idea of the good life is a week in Honolulu" may be too long, so try "Sleeping as late as I want is a big part of the good life."
As a rule, dive deep into a subject:

Watching a movie with my boyfriend is part of the good life for me. When the lights in the theater dim and everybody stops talking, it's just like being at a lake when the wind stops and the water gets smooth and quiet. I reach for Tom with one hand and with the other I choose one perfect, completely buttered kernel of popcorn and slowly raise it to my lips.

Assignment 16

As far as education goes, what do you think is the difference between teaching and indoctrination?

Comment: This assignment asks you to define a couple of words. But don't go running to the dictionary! Writing problems like this need real experiences to define fat, abstract words. Sure, a dictionary can define *foolish*, but until you've forked over your hard-earned cash to a fast-talking salesman, you don't really know what the word means.

Let's look at indoctrination, the second of the key words, first. Probably you've had a teacher who thought his or her way was the only way. If you were beaten up with that point of view, you were indoctrinated. But most of us have had teachers who presented options. They said, in effect, "There is more than one way of looking at this issue. Here are the facts as we know them. What do you think?"

Here's a sample thesis that could be modified to get into this assignment comfortably: "Mr. Penfield taught me how to use psychology, but Mrs. Walker just indoctrinated me about history." Sometimes writing with pictures can help a reader to see what you're driving at. Here is a seeable thesis sentence that does just that:

Indoctrination is like this: all the students go into class carrying a piece of white paper, and they all come out with the paper tinted the same color. Teaching, though, sends them out with papers of all different colors.

Assignment 17

"You're not a woman until you've had children." Discuss this quotation briefly.

Comment: This feels like another exercise in Definition. It asks you to define *woman* by discussing the part that children play in the definition. You're asked only to "discuss briefly," so it will be a short paper on a large topic, what cowboys used to call a tall order. Here are some samples to get you started thinking:

I think any female over the age of eighteen is a woman, but until she has had a child, she's not complete. Men have their work and women have their children.

To equate womanhood with motherhood is as silly as saying, "You're not a man unless you smoke Nails." Nobody would fall for that advertisement, and nobody should fall for this version of it, either.

I know that the quotation is old-fashioned, but I still think there's something to it. Good jobs, good friends, and good relationships might make a good person, but children are what make a woman.

Perhaps these will give you some ideas for your own opening sentences. Don't worry about being perfect and satisfying every reader. Be honest and tell the truth as you see and feel it.

Assignment 18

If you don't measure success in monetary terms, how do you measure it?

Comment: There are two options built right into the thesis. The first is to say, "I do measure success in monetary terms." Then go on to show how Cadillacs, condos, and Convair jets are the symbols of a successful man or woman. But if you don't measure success by how much money a person makes or spends, then your job is to say how you do measure it. Say it. Don't dance around it. Don't write this kind of prose:

Money isn't everything, and success can be measured in other ways. Lots of successful people aren't rich but they still feel good about themselves and are "successes" in different ways than the rich man or movie star.

Somewhere a reader is screaming, "Get to the point!" If you measure success not by money but by happiness, say so. If you measure it by contentment or peace of mind, say that. Then go on to vividly and realistically show your reader exactly what you mean.
Here is a student's paper with a promising beginning:

I measure success by how well-liked a person is. My Aunt Edna never made more than $12,000 a year in her life working as a seamstress, but she had dozens of customers who became her friends.

Assignment 19

If someone wanted to become a failure, what qualities does he or she need?

Comment: Here is a topic that's easy to misunderstand, so read the assignment again, please. You're being asked to write about the qualities that are essential for failure. Don't feel compelled to lecture on success or to criticize failure.
The thesis can be very direct: "In order to fail, a person should be _____ and _____." You might fill in the blanks with anything that makes sense: selfish and mean, snotty and bad-tempered, or lazy and critical. You need at least two qualities because one of the key words — *qualities* — is plural.
Most assignments in writing classes are, I admit, serious, but it's also okay to have fun with them with it's appropriate:

I think poor taste and bad judgment should qualify almost anyone for failure. Marching into a memorial service wearing a glow-in-the-dark orange suit and bright green socks should get things started. Or coughing into the minister's face and telling his wife the joke about the gorilla and the missionary should move the evening right along.

Assignment 20

If you could begin next year with one new ability, what would it be?

Comment: Although this looks straightforward enough, it can be misunderstood. *Ability* is the key word, so manipulate your thesis accordingly. An ability usually means being able to do something like study better, run faster, or understand more thoroughly. So if you want to start the new year being cuter, be careful how you compose (as in Composition 1A) your thesis. For most people, beauty isn't an ability. A clever person, though, might say, "I'd like to begin next year by being able to attract girls easier."
I've talked before about being vivid and specific as you develop your paragraphs or short essays, and I've talked about how the thesis is always the biggest generalization while all the other supporting sentences are more real and concrete. See if this example will help: You go into a restaurant and say, "I want something to eat, please." That's the thesis. What follows should move from the general to the specific.

I want something to eat, please. I want Lipton's tea, a small steak done medium rare, a baked potato with sour cream, green beans, apple pie, and coffee with cream.

As you write about the new ability you may begin next year with, be a good diner. Tell your reader exactly what you have on your mind.

Assignment 21

"The United States is a nation of disposable heroes." In a paragraph of not more than one hundred words, agree or disagree with this statement.

Comment: With only a hundred words to work with, you might simply give examples of heroes who are or are not disposable. If you choose Abraham Lincoln or Joe Dimaggio, they've been around long enough to show how some heroes are nearly permanent. If you pick TV stars or hot guitar players, they're liable to be replaced next month.

There's nothing wrong with the paragraph that simply names names and that says, in effect, "Look. Most of us will never forget people like John F. Kennedy and Martin Luther King, and here are some reasons why." There is also the paragraph that comes from other angles:

Since the U.S. can dispose of everything from beer cans to diapers, it only makes sense that   our heroes would be disposable, too.

I just want to remind everyone again that there is rarely a right or wrong answer to any assignment. How you express and support what you feel is what counts. That's why one student can say that America's heroes are disposable, another can claim America's heroes are not, and *they can both write strong papers.*

Assignment 22

What really scared you when you were a kid?

Comment: The last few assignments have been to discuss or argue or explain. This one asks you to describe and to make the reader see and feel. Here are some more ways to think about the assignment: What story gave you the creeps? What bully made you never want to leave the house again?
The real key to this is to remember that the reader should be as scared as you were! That won't happen by just saying, "When I woke up at midnight, I was always scared." You need to be more vivid: "When I woke up and all the lights in the house were off, I was sure there were slimy monsters under the bed."
Here are a couple of openings to look at. The first one isn't bad, but the second one is better.

This kid in grade school, Mark Columbo, really scared me. He was this bully. He was only eleven, but he was huge. If that wasn't bad enough, he was ugly. And he was always threatening me.

In grade school, a kid named Mark Columbo really scared me. We were both in sixth grade, but Mark weighed at least 160. We played touch football at recess, and Mark liked to pick on me. He'd run over me, then jog back, lean down with snot coming out of his fat, piggy nose and snarl, "I'm gonna git you after school, dork brain."

Assignment 23

Describe your ideal room.

Comment: In Exposition a reader follows as you explain; in Argumentation he tracks your reasoning; in Description he sees. In Description, then, you're a lot like a camera. So be like a camera. Don't say only *pretty, comfy, bright* or *fabulous*. Say that the room is *sun-drenched*, that the sofa is *cushiony*, and that the chairs are *canary-yellow*. Cameras can't record fat words like *pretty*, so be a camera and record what it sees.

Take a color picture of this ideal room. What do you see out the windows? Which books do you want in the shelves? What paintings, posters, prints are on the wall? What color rug is in there? What kind of furniture, and what does it look like?

Since a paragraph is developed by adding details until the promise in the thesis is kept (the thesis here is a promise to describe your ideal room), it's clear that the details that add up to comfort, for example, are going to be different from those that add up to beauty.

The words in a thesis are not like the freight cars in a long train where one or two more or less won't make that much difference. Words in a thesis are much more like the chemicals in a formula for Chemistry II. If you change one of the ingredients, the whole thing changes. Luckily, in writing you can't blow yourself up!

Assignment 24

Discuss the reality that television is broadcasting into our living rooms.

Comment: Here is a classic Expository assignment. It's a mistake, then, to slip into criticisms and judgments about television and to turn this into an Argumentative paper. You might get away with it, but many teachers will hold you right to the assignment, and one of the things this book teaches is to read carefully and see exactly what you're asked to do.

I'd be very careful about tackling all of television. From the first pages, I've been talking about limiting thesis sentences so the your essays or paragraphs feel complete. All of television is just too much; that feels more like a book. Also, don't forget to name names. Say "Hard Copy." Say "Donahue." Name the characters, the advertisements, or the products they're selling. Don't be satisfied with sentences that don't go any farther than this one: "Some ads show things that just aren't real." Make your explanations vivid: "No one really believes that a Ford Bronco can drive straight up a glacier."
Here are three different thesis sentences to play with:

The reality of soap operas is nothing but lying, infidelity, and passion.

The nightly news offers a very grim reality since it suggests that the important things in life are the tragedies and the disasters.

I don't believe TV is broadcasting any kind of reality, since even a kid knows TV isn't real.

Assignment 25

"Much of the reality that television projects is a negative one."
Agree or disagree.

Comment: This assignment should help you see the difference in Exposition and Argumentation since it's essentially the same as #24. But this time there is a different intent: to convince, not merely just discuss.

An Expository paragraph from #24 might read something like this:

The reality of most soap operas is a lot more intense than mine. I come home from work, cook some paghetti for dinner, and watch "Monday Night Football." But not the guys on "Whirling World." Old Baxter comes out of a coma and learns that birthmark on his wrist means he's actually King of Prussia.

But the thesis for #25 should concentrate on the negative aspects of soap operas. Here are two possible theses:

The reality of a soap opera like "Whirling World" is so steamy and intense that it could seduce someone into thinking that lying and infidelity are always part of life."

Advertisements exaggerate or lie, nightly news is tragic so people will stay tuned, and dramatic shows feature rape, incest, and murder. Who could possibly claim that TV is anything but negative?

Assignment 26

What do you think it means to be well-informed?

Comment: I think students should take at least three steps into an assignment like this. First, feel the obvious essay. And that, in this case, is one about reading newspapers and magazines, watching the network news, and generally keeping up with what's happening. This essay could mention *Time* or *U.S. News and World Report*. It could name some news commentators who are usually trustworthy. All that's fine, as far as it goes.

The next step, though, is to at least consider this question: well-informed about what? Being well-informed about money matters is different from being well-informed about politics. Can all of this, and more, be in one short paper?

Finally, consider how much editing goes on before we read or hear the news. Do you think that some things are left out? Even if a person wants to be well-informed and does her best, do you think she's getting all the news all the time? If not, then what does well-informed actually mean?
 If you're stuck on this one and if it's okay with your teacher, just use this thesis and fill in the blanks: "To be well-informed about _____,   I'd have to _____."

Assignment 27

Do you think it's true that absence makes the heart grow fonder, or when the cat's away do the mice just play?

Comment: This assignment asks you to evaluate a couple of old-fashioned proverbs in the light of your own experience. Of course, you may use others' experiences, too. How did your friend act when her boyfriend went away? What was your aunt like when your uncle got drafted? What did Bruce do on weekends when Trixie went to Malibu for the summer? There are actually three options here, not just two. Your thesis might say that absence actually does make the heart grow fonder. Or it might claim that the person left alone just parties. Or it might argue that both proverbs can be true under different circumstances.

If your teacher doesn't assign a definite length, ask yourself how long a writer can go on about a subject like this. Most topics have a built-in limit. "Why I Hate My Sister Leslie" is finished when readers say to themselves, "Lord, Leslie is a brat. No wonder he hates her." "Three Ways to Save Money" is over when the three ways have been explained. What about this one?

Get a thesis that you like; then write solid, direct prose. Don't be content with sentences like this: "People go away and they feel different about those they leave behind." Rather, "When my friend Bob left his fiancee for a weekend trip to Las Vegas, the first thing he did was fall in love with a dancer in the Follies."

Assignment 28

Pick a commercial that you just love or hate and discuss the qualities that make you feel so strongly.

Comment: Any time a thesis gives you trouble, go back to basics: "I love (or hate) the commercial for _____ because _____." Of course every thesis for every paper doesn't have to be so cut and dried, but this book intends to give you a few things you can depend on when it comes to writing for teachers.

Readers have to see and feel why you feel so strongly about some commercial. They have to experience the charm or music or energy right along with you. That's why an opening like this isn't very good:

I hate the commercial for Boom Boom Detergent because it's boring. It doesn't really tell me anything about the product, and it puts me to sleep every time. I can't believe the company thinks this boring commercial is any good. It isn't. It's just dull.

The thesis here is promising enough, but then the writer goes on automatic pilot, and he writes a boring paragraph about boredom. Big mistake. The reader has to hear the droning announcer, see the hypnotic sloshing of the washer and endure the zombie-like mother folding, folding, endlessly folding.

Assignment 29

What is the most frustrating thing that regularly happens to you?

Comment: Here is a sample paragraph on this topic:

Holding On By My Fingernails

Calling on the phone and being put on Hold is very frustrating for me. I called the gas company a few days ago, and a recorded message asked me to be patient. Then I listened to a Muzak version of "I Want to Hold Your Hand" for about five minutes. After that, another recorded voice said,"Our operators are still busy. Please hold the line." I held on during more watered-down Beatles as I stared out the window, shifted the phone from ear to ear and chewed on a fingernail. Other people might not want to scream when they're put on Hold, but I do. It's just about the most frustrating thing in the world.

For most teachers this is a good paragraph. It starts right in, gives the examples and gets right out. It sticks to the topic and feels like it was written by a real person.
It is also harder to write than it looks! So if your paragraphs don't come out as vivid or as smooth at first, don't be discouraged.

Assignment 30

What's the difference between self-confidence and self-esteem?

Comment: This assignment calls for a kind of development called Comparison/Contrast. This isn't a type of writing like Exposition or Argumentation, but another way to make any type of writing clear and believable.

A funny thing about writing is that students usually do the right thing without even thinking about it. Someone trying to get his dad to loan him the family car doesn't just explain (Exposition) his need, he argues for it: "But, Dad, I've never had an accident of any kind and I always fill up the tank!" Someone telling about a tragedy doesn't just say it happened, he describes it: "God, there was blood everywhere and a piece of the fender was sticking through her ankle."

For this assignment, try to stay away from philosophy and theory, and write about a self- confident person who is actually doing something. Then compare him or her to another person who has self-esteem. For example, how does a woman who is confident act on a job interview compared to one who thinks highly of herself?

Or pick a man who just acts self-confident and compare him to another man who actually has self-esteem.

Assignment 31

What's the difference between aggressive and assertive?

Comment: Suppose this assignment were easier and you only had to compare the school you're at now with an earlier one. Maybe you'd decide to compare the teachers, the cafeteria food, or the parking problems in the student lots. Here's an example:

At Washington High School the were generally helpful. Mr. Wilson in math stayed late to help me solve some hard problems and Mrs. Mendoza, my English teacher, gave me extra work that would bring up my grades. At college, though, the teachers seem pretty heartless. Mostly they just say, "Work harder." When I asked my biology teacher what I could do to get a better grade he said that he was busy but maybe I could see him on his office hour.

Even though showing the difference between assertive and aggressive seems harder, the general idea is the same. Since it was possible to show the differences between two schools by naming names and giving examples, name names and give examples here, too. Choose a situation or two and show how an aggressive person might act compared to an assertive one. How does an aggressive guy buy tickets to a concert compared to an assertive one? How do they ask for a date, talk to a cop, or order a hamburger?

Assignment 32

People make a living criticizing films for newspapers and magazines, and almost all of us talk or argue about the movies we've seen. In a short paper, discuss the qualities that a film has to have before you are willing to say that it's good.

Comment: This isn't a trick question, but it does have a tricky key word — *good*. It's too hazy for my tastes, and it means too many different things to too many people. But there it is, so let's work with it.

First, I wouldn't use the key word very many times. Sentences like this don't really move the paper along: "A good movie to me has to have good actors and a lot of good action." That thesis might be salvaged, though, with only a few changes :

A good movie has to have actual movie stars and lots of excitement. Give me Robert Redford on horseback running away from the posse in *Butch Cassidy and the Sundance Kid* or Clint Eastwood prowling the alleys of New York with his Magnum.

Next, choose actual qualities like action, suspense, a message, attractive characters in small costumes, or gallons of blood. I wouldn't, by the way, try and impress anybody by being phony. If your idea of a good movie is one where six Cadillacs chase each other for twenty minutes and then crash and burn, say so.

Finally, don't forget to name some films. In the heat of writing, we all forget that readers need something real to hold onto.

Assignment 33

What does it mean to be cool?\

Comment: This assignment looks like another one in
Definition. Yet someone could argue that it's an Expository
paper in which *cool* is simply explained. Who's right?

Both are right. The only reason to know the names for things is
to make life easier, not harder. Probably Adam named the
animals so he and Eve could chat without pointing and drawing
pictures in the dirt. In this assignment, an impulse to Explain is
just as good as one to Define as long as the reader ends up feeling
what it means to be cool. Take a look at a few possible thesis
sentences —

1. Being cool is mostly an attitude.
2. Cool people never crack under pressure.
3. There are different kinds of cool.

The first seems hardest to develop, since <u>attitude</u> is just another
word to define or explain. It can be done, though, and a good
start is to show someone in hundred dollar Ray Ban shades and
a sneer. The second should develop with a few examples:
people taking exams, talking to angry bosses, or being
interviewed for a big job. In #3, comparing/contrasting should
do the job as you show the differences between being cool at
fourteen and at twenty-four or the difference between being cool
among men compared to being cool among women.

Which is best? Well, writing isn't like math. There are lots of
right answers. Writing is like traveling; there is more than one
way to get where you're going.

Assignment 34

In what ways are the huge shopping malls on the outskirts of town actually like the downtown shopping areas they've replaced?

Comment: Maybe some background will help here. As little as twenty years ago, small towns had one street. The stores faced one another across Main St. like neighbors chatting over a back fence. When malls were built, however, the novelty, convenience and comfort drew people away from downtown. The assignment asks only for a short discussion of how two things that seem to be different are really the same. So a straight answer will do. For example, "Although they do look different, malls are just like Main St. because they both want to attract customers, and they both want to make money." There is also this sort of opening:

The similarities of the mall and downtown are only on the surface. Sure, both have customers and both sell things. But that's where it ends. Malls are cold and the clerks are strangers. Downtowns used to be   warm and everybody knew everybody else.

Experiment with a few thesis sentences. Be like the stores you're writing about. Spruce up flat, expository prose with some window dressing. Don't settle for mall and Main St. all the time. Say Miller's Outpost, The Gap and Supercuts compared to Jerry's Toggery, Sam's Style Shop and Nancy's Beauty Nook.

Assignment 35

Do you think the loss of the traditional downtown shopping area is a real loss? If so, what exactly is lost? Or are the changes simply inevitable and part of an on-going process that isn't necessarily a bad thing?

Comment: This is a much more interesting assignment than #34. It goes wider and deeper; it's much less cool and removed. Here are some possible thesis sentences:

1. I think the loss of the old-fashioned downtowns is a tragedy because a whole way of life goes, too.
2. Just thinking about the change in a practical way there's a real loss because family businesses collapse and long-time employees are laid off.

3. Some things change when a mall replaces Main St., but movies come and go, hemlines rise and fall, and people are born and die.

4. Like it or not, progress is inevitable. And the new malls with more convenience, lower prices, and greater comfort are part of that progress.

An assignment like this lets you be yourself. If you're feeling sentimental, you might want to ask how anyone could prefer the artificiality of the mall. On the other hand a practical person just likes to get all the shopping down quickly. Both essays are "right."

Assignment 36

Why do some people spend a lot of money to buy uncomfortable and sometimes unattractive fashions?

Comment: Assignments beginning with *Why* usually need only a sensible reason or two to satisfy most writing teachers. No one really knows for sure why fashion-conscious people go to the limit on their VISA cards for tight coats with three sleeves, so what amounts to a good guess will do.
Consider the key words *uncomfortable* and *unattractive*. It's easy to assume we all know what they mean, but that isn't true. Like a lot of words — *love,* for example — they mean different things to different people. In fact, one of the tricks to always writing well is to make surea reader knows what you mean by your key words. For *unattractive,* consider a descriptive sentence like this: "His red pants were so tight, he couldn't breathe, and they ended above his green socks."

Don't lose sight of the basic assignment; don't forget to answer the question. If no reasons for people's weird and expensive tastes bubble up to the top of yours minds, here are some things that other students have thought of — to be accepted, to fit in, to be different, to be looked at, to feel important, to get attention, to impress somebody.

Finally, remind yourself of the assignment's length. Which reason or reasons appeal to you most? Then ask yourself which you can write the most about.

Assignment 37

Why do boys seldom take jobs as baby-sitters?

Comment: A clever student could probably write a paragraph on this assignment in fifteen minutes or less. He or she might logically say that boys don't baby-sit because they aren't offered jobs as baby sitters. Or someone might simply point out that boys don't baby-sit because their friends don't. Both of these reasons seem valid to me, and I can easily imagine the developed paragraph.

This is also a chance to write a more distinguished essay, one with a little more meat on its bones. Let me suggest a few things:
Do you think there is just something about boys that disqualifies them as baby-sitters? What would that something be, and how could you pin it down in an essay? Were they born with it — an anti-baby-sitting gene — or is it something they learned?

If they were born with or without it, how could you show this? If it's something they learned, where did they learn it? Did games teach them to be too rough? Did TV make them too aggressive? Did their heroes or role models convince them that real men don't change diapers.

Teachers who grade heavily on Content often explain to their classes that the obvious answers to Why assignments usually aren't rewarded because they're obvious; each essay looks pretty much like its neighbor. So if one of my questions will help set your paper off from the others, help yourself.

Assignment 38

The television industry survives by selling time to advertisers, and they prosper when consumers buy the advertised products. Do you ever feel that quality has been sacrificed in order to accommodate advertisers, or are you generally satisfied by the quality of the shows you watch?

Comment: One person's entertaining half-hour is another's thirty-minute bore. "Wheel of Fortune" charms and relaxes some people; others think it's a disgrace. The question is this: what do you mean by *quality*?
In writing, no one can tell you what to like. You're free to enjoy "Watching Plants Grow." But you have to be willing to say, "Watching Plants Grow" is my idea of a good show because it's non-violent and free from racial stereotypes." You must commit yourself. Key words (in this case its *quality*) have to be understood exactly as the writer means them. And they mean different things to all of us. Even if we all know what gray means, there are different shades of that.

If you feel TV is pretty much free of advertiser influence, your paper simply explains of how good t.v. is and how unlikely it is that advertisers have much say in what is or is not shown. If, on the other hand, you feel that billion dollar accounts do affect the quality of the media, showing this is essential.
Obviously, very few of us will have the evidence to prove that Kodak or Chrysler has convinced NBC to cancel a certain show, but most of us can imagine what it would take to panic most executives. What could make Ford Motor Co. or Proctor & Gamble threaten to not buy ten million dollars worth of air time?

Assignment 39

If you could wake up tomorrow as someone else, who would it be?

Comment: Questions like these — and they're sprinkled through books like mine — have a probing nature, and the best essays are willing to talk about the values that the questions turn up.

If, for example, the thesis is this, "I'd like to wake up as Robert Redford," the person values good looks, charisma, and the whole movie star package. "I'd like to wake up as the President," on the other hand, suggests a taste for global influence and power. "I'd like to be Robin Hood" shows someone who would like to right some wrongs and live in the forest with a bunch of guys.

Be very clear about the values built into the person you choose. Your reader may be able to figure them out as he reads, but it's always best to be precise.

This is an assignment to have some fun with. It's fine to want to wake up as Florence Nightingale or Mother Theresa; it's more fun to want to be a monster: "I'd like to wake up as Dracula because he gets to stay out all night and his parents never get mad and take away his car."

Most students get caught up in the seriousness of writing for grades. Teachers — most of us, anyway — are human, too. Make yours smile once in a while.

Assignment 40

How much do you think class size has to do with how well students learn? Naturally students' motivation and teachers' skills have a lot to do with learning, but for the sake of this paper, concentrate on class size.

Comment: This book teaches young writers to look closely at their assignments (any assignments in any class) and to see exactly what's being asked. This one wants to know how much, and the answer may be anywhere between very little and a lot.

Variables like motivation and skill have been weeded out, so what are your experiences with large and small classes? Are they representative enough to make a readable paper? If they're personally eccentric or downright weird, are you willing to modify them in order to sound more convincing?

I think it's always wise to know what the standard essay is for each assignment, the essay that, over the years, most people have written most of the time. Here it's probably the one about students learning more in small classes because each person gets more attention.

There's nothing wrong with that essay. And, knowing what it is, you're also in a position to write a different one if you have the time or energy. For example, it's certainly possible that in some large classes, students help each other. And in some small ones, the slower kids stand out more, get discouraged and learn even less.

Knowing the standard essay, you're in charge. You can try anything that appeals to you.

Assignment 41

How often should a person be given another chance after he has been unfaithful, lied, or broken a promise?

Comment: Writing assignments aren't tricky because teachers are mean people with nothing better to do than torture students. They're tricky because sorting out the key words and creating a thesis usually takes some work.

Here, for example, the little word *or* makes a world of difference in how long the paper is and what direction it takes. Having it in the assignment means you may write about infidelity or lying or breaking promises, but not necessarily all three. And it can't be wise to lump them all together. Realistically, sexual infidelity has shattered a lot of marriages while breaking promises about picking up dirty socks has just caused some fights.

Always be specific! Exactly what kinds of lies and promises are you writing about? What sort of promises have to be broken? And to whom or what has someone been unfaithful?

I know the tendency in assignments like this is to give a number — once, three times or six times — but it's also possible to truthfully say, "It depends on the circumstances," and to develop that. There are even teachers who would insist on this approach, arguing that it's naive to try and pin a number on emotional things.

Assignment 42

Some doctors now believe that people make themselves sick with their attitudes and life styles. How much do you think people have to do with their own health?

Comment: Here is another how much problem, so the thesis needs a good guess (very little, some, plenty) followed by believable specifics and examples.
Take a look at an opening that might sound okay but probably isn't:

People can influence their health enormously.Positive thinking can help people be well, just like negative thinking can make them sick. Illness doesn't just come out of nowhere. People invite it with their thinking and lifestyles.

Compare that to this:

I know that when I'm tired or depressed or both, I'm more likely to get a cold or flu than when I'm not. I'm nearly always flat on my back in bed during exams because I'm a worrier and worrying takes a lot of energy.

The second writer wisely limited her examples to the person she knew the most about — herself — while the first one seemed to be giving someone a pep talk instead of developing a paragraph.

Assignment 43

Assume that there are class distinctions in the United States, and write about the differences among the upper, middle, and lower classes.

Comment: There should be a big DANGER sign on assignments like this, because they can be fouled up so easily. Books have been written on this topic, so be prepared to show some real restraint. Here are some things to ponder.

Should you write about how the different classes think, about how different their clothes are, or about the differences in their cars? Is it fair to say that classes can be symbolized by things like champagne, wine, and beer? If so, can you make the same distinction using cars, food, parts of the country, or politics? Is there a religion of the upper class, a middle class soft drink, or a lower class hobby? Can you make class distinctions by looking at people's haircuts or clothes? Are there attitudes built into different classes? For example, how do the upper classes feel about abortion or capital punishment compared to the lower? How do you know they feel this way?

The assignment asks you to discuss, so you may explain, criticize or amuse, too. "I can tell the differences among the classes by how they hold their hamburgers" might get the point across just as well as a more ponderous thesis.

Whatever you do with this one, don't try too much!

Assignment 44

What's the biggest mistake you can make on a first date?

Comment: One way to write well is to start by looking for the danger in each assignment, like a member of the Bomb Squad checking out the building first. In an Argument, the logic could be faulty. In Exposition, the facts might be dreary, and in Description the pictures could turn out murky.
What's the danger here? My guess would be too long a paper or too much seriousness. I don't think it's fair to tell students to be funny like being funny was something anybody could do on command. School usually isn't a funny institution, and sitting in rows with the clock ticking isn't a lot of laughs. But you can step back a little and use the lightest touch you have at the moment to write something short and sweet.

Would a list of the things that might go wrong help? Being late picking up your date, mistaking her mom for her dad ("How do you do, Mr. Jones. Whoops!"), being late getting her home and meeting the Missing Persons Patrol on her doorstep, being dressed for a beach party and being taken to a formal dinner, going to sleep while you're parked in the moonlight.

Notice, by the way, how most of the things in the list are from a man's point of view. Just for fun, try turning things around. Women have bad first dates, too. How are they different from a man's?

Assignment 45

Everybody from musicians to the President's wife urges kids to stay in high school and graduate. Do you think it's important for teenagers to graduate because they need to learn certain skills, facts or attitudes, or do you think that graduation is just a symbol to people (especially employers) that here's a young person who can finish something?

Comment: This is another either/or problem, so be prepared to commit yourself. If you choose skills, facts or attitudes, you must name some. Are you talking about being able to write standard English and balance a checkbook, or are there other skills? What facts would make it worthwhile for a restless student to stick it out and graduate? If not the dates of the World Wars or Lincoln's inauguration, what about the facts of life? Here are three different thesis sentences to get you started.

Graduation better be a symbolic act, because the attitudes I learned, namely popularity-at-all-costs and conformity, are either useless, dangerous, or both.

I think high school is mostly a proving ground for employers who figure that anybody who has the stamina and discipline to get through four years can probably hack it with them, too."

High school taught me to get along with cranky teachers, hostile gangs, and oversexed boys, so I graduated with plenty of skills to survive in the real world.

Assignment 46

Do you think it would be fun to live a constantly exciting life?

Comment: This doesn't seem like that hard an assignment as assignments go, but it has its tricky spots. All of us have distinct ideas about what fun is. I like to bet on horses; others get a kick out of church picnics. What does the word *fun* mean to you in this context? *Exciting* is another problem. Does it mean new things (what things?) all the time, or the same things in ever-increasing amounts?

By now you're used to adjusting thesis sentences, so you know the easy one here is the direct approach: "Yes, I think it'd be fun to live a constantly exciting life. I love to race cars, and driving a Porche in races all over the world would never bore me." Consider, though, taking no for an answer. "No, I wouldn't like constant excitement. It'd be too much like being awake all the time. Like night comes after day, I need some time to think and recover."

What if you feel one way but think you can write a stronger paper by taking the other side? What if you don't really like excitement, but you think you can write a pretty good paper about sky-diving? Is that dishonest? Most of us don't feel like going to work every day, but we do. Writing is your job; do it the best way you can.

Assignment 47

Is it possible to have too much beauty, too much good luck, or too much money?

Comment: Everyone knows the story about the unhappy movie star, the bored lottery winner, and the spoiled rich kid. It's possible to write about them since it's probably true that people with striking physical beauty often feel desired only for how they look; it wouldn't be fun to win every bet every time; and being able to buy anything would make shopping pretty weird. Yet, would you sit through another movie about a model who yearned to be liked for her mind?

I know it sounds strange to say to a young writer, "You can take this approach to the assignment and probably get a decent grade, but do you really want to?" The fact is, though, that this book and these little chats are supposed to give students more options. If this were a text for a cooking school, I'd still say,

"You can probably make ham and eggs again and pass the Breakfast exam, but at least consider another dish."

Try a few different things. If nothing works, there's always ham and eggs, which are delicious.

Assignment 48

Students are sometimes herded to assemblies to hear poets, actors, string quartets or lecturers. Do you think it's educational at all to be subjected to culture, or are these performances mostly a waste of time?

Comment: Nearly all assignments have a bias; let's look at this one. Notice some of the words and phrases: "Herded," for example, implying sheep or cows. Then there's "subjected to culture." Would "exposed to culture" have made a difference? Notice the fat, abstract words like *culture* and *educational*.

Now that we've decided the water is muddy, let's see if we can use it, anyway. The basic question is this: Is there anything educational about seeing poets, actors, musicians or speakers, or are performances like these pointless?

I think seeing actors is educational. In grade school, a Shakespeare company came to my school. Everybody giggled at the guys in tights, but I never forgot the way they stopped after each scene and explained how the words worked.

I think it's mostly a waste of time to expose students to culture. Exposed is an odd word, anyway. Are students supposed to be infected by music like a cold or the flu? All the kids that I know who like classical music have always liked it. They didn't get infected in any assembly.

Sit with these two different paragraphs for a little bit. Is the one you prefer true or just written better?

Assignment 49

Can important decisions can be based on intuition rather than logic?

Comment: The key words, *intuition* and *logic,* are easy enough to see. And the paragraph's or essay's focus has to be on "important decisions." So buying socks won't do. Buying a car will.
Here is an opening that doesn't get the job done. Its nose is too high in the air:

Feeling can't do the job that logic can when it comes to important decisions. Feelings are only sensations or impulses. They aren't as trustworthy as facts. What if everybody went around feeling and not thinking?

Here is one that's more down to earth:

I've done all right trusting my feelings. When I started going with Ruthie, my feelings told me I was right. Logically, she wasn't a beauty queen, and she wasn't rich or brainy. But my logical friends have broken up with their logical girlfriends, and Ruth and I are still happy.

Don't forget that either/or is not the only option, either. How about a thesis that suggested some decisions are best left to logic, others to feelings, and still others to a combination of both head and heart.

Assignment 50

If you could have one new skill for a year, what would it be?

Comment: As you investigate this question, isolating the key words and seeing exactly what the assignment is looking for, let me say a few words about the difference between paragraphs and essays.

If you were asked to write a paragraph on this topic, the thesis might look like this: "For a year I'd like to be able to understand stock market options so I could make a lot of money." A few examples of the mysteries of Wall St. would develop that thesis.

But what if the assignment is to write anything longer than a paragraph? Then the thesis has to change, too. For example: "For a year I'd like to have enough insight to understand why people act the way they do." Now the writer can go on to discuss why people get married six times, hurt one another, start wars, tell jokes, pollute, and pray. It might be a very long essay. What if he'd said, "I want enough insight to understand why people are sometimes cruel"?   That paper is shorter since he's only going to ponder just one aspect of human behavior.

Not everyone can fit into the same clothes. Even suits right off the rack come in different sizes because our bodies are different. Well, so are our ideas and our ways of talking about them. One thesis needs only half a dozen crisp sentences to be developed; another needs three paragraphs or five.

Try for the stylish but comfortable thesis, the one that fits best and is right for the occasion.

Assignment 51

When was the last time you changed your mind about something after reading a book or article or listening to a debate?

Comment: Here is an Expository paper about the merits of Argumentation. That's quirky enough for me to like.

The assignment is direct, and the obvious essay begins with the obvious answer. "A year ago I changed my mind about voting for Mr. X when I read about his underworld connections." Then it goes on to graphically explain how warm feelings toward X cooled.

Notice that a thesis like this won't work: "I changed my mind about Tom after I caught him with another girl." Unless the writer read about sneaky old Tom in *Newsweek* or heard his character debated on "Firing Line," she isn't reading the assignment carefully.

There is another possibility. "I've never changed my mind about anything important after just reading a book or listening to a debate." *Important* is a terrific choice of words for this thesis. Now we know the writer may have been convinced to switch brands of detergent or buy a Pontiac instead of a Honda, but she hasn't been swayed yet from her feelings about capital punishment, birth control, abortion, or the United Nations.

Assignment 52

What does it mean to act like a man, and is there anything dangerous about urging boys to do this?

Comment: Although the thesis might seem long, I'd at least try and get everything in. "Acting like a man means being strong, not giving up and sticking out the tough times, and the danger is teaching this to boys who aren't mature enough." Or, "Real men stand behind their friends, protect their wives and children, and don't cry about things, and that's not dangerous."

Either way, the effectiveness of the examples will make the essays more or less attractive and readable. Here is the beginning of a promising essay. Not so much because of what it says, but how it says it:

Acting like a man means, among other things, being tolerant. A man can have an opinion and respect someone else's opinion, too. Maybe I hate communism, but somebody can still read Karl Marx if he wants to. A boy, however, always has to have things his way.

Assignment 53

If you could change your first name, what would you change it to?

Comment: Since "I'd call myself Lance" isn't an essay, there's a built-in *Why*? in assignments like this. Why would you change your name to Lance, Trixi, Molly or Skipper?

An acceptable paragraph can grow out of this assignment as long as it's either honest or at least sounds honest. Here are a few thesis sentences to give you some ideas:

I'd change my name from Yvette to Mary because Yvette sounds so French that it embarrasses me.

My nickname is Squeaky, and I'd give anything to change it to Thor or Rocky.

My last name is Kiltz. I'd like to change it to Gilliam because I'm sick of jokes about Kilts and Silt and Klutz. Gilliam is easy to pronounce but not too common.

My name is William, just like my dad's, and I'd like to change it to anything else because I'm tired of being Little Willy and living in my dad's shadow.

Assignment 54

On the wall of a famous department store in Texas is this brass plaque: At The End, The One With The Most Toys Wins. Do you think this is another disheartening example of greed and competitiveness or merely a light-hearted approach to life that shouldn't be taken too seriously?

Comment: I think the motto is awful. It stands for everything heartless and selfish about Americans, especially how we think that things are more important than people.

I can't believe anybody would take a store's slogan too seriously. Do people really think that things Go Better With Coke? Does anybody actually belong to The Pepsi Generation?

Now it's also time to ask yourself, "Okay, I'm against X, but I'll bet I write a stronger paper being for it."
Some students say, "I'm so strongly opposed to X that I could never write anything that was in favor of it." Others reply, "Well, I feel strongly about X, too; but given the assignment and the time I have, I'm better off leaning the other way."

You're not cheating or lying. You're writing the best essay you can.

Assignment 55

What is one of the worst things that people do to one another?

Comment: This assignment sounds personal, but people also start wars and commit genocide as well as deceive, lie, rape and kill.
 Beware of trying to let the scary key word do all the work. Here, for example, are some weak lines about infidelity:

When women find out their husbands have been unfaithful, it really hits them hard. The news is so unexpected, they don't know what to do. They are so sick at heart and hurt by their unfaithful husbands.

Compare these:

Being unfaithful is one of the worst things a man can do to a woman. When a friend of mine, Marge, found out that her husband was seeing someone else, she just went to pieces. Dishes piled up in the sink, she cried like someone had died, and just wandered around the house all day in her nightgown.

Was there really a friend named Marge, or did the writer decide to invent one in order to make his point in a dramatic and moving way? We'll never know for sure, yet the second example is much sharper than the first.

Assignment 56

What does someone have to do to earn your respect?

Comment: The thesis can be absolutely direct. "Someone has to
_____ to earn my respect." The blank could be filled in
various ways, from the very general (stand up for what's right)
to the specific (fight me and win).

Here is another way to approach this writing problem: "I respect
_____ because he or she _____."
Look at some possibilities:

I respect my mom because she holds our family together.

I respect anyone who sticks by his principles.

I respect my doctor because he's a real healer.

I respect the President because his job is so hard.

I respect Magic Johnson because he's the kind of athlete and the
kind of man I'd like to be.

Each of these thesis sentences begins a different sized paper since
the various key words and phrases need different kinds of
information in different amounts to make them clear.
Photographs sit in the darkroom and develop at the same time
no matter how complicated the picture is; essays aren't like that.
They need varying amounts of time and work to be understood
completely.

Focus your paper on respect. Remember that the assignment
asks what someone does, not what he is or believes in.

Assignment 57

If you could create a new religion, what would it be like?

Comment: Although this looks like an essay that could go on until it became a theology text, it could easily be limited to a paragraph. It might be serious: "My new religion needs just one thing — a God who is female." Or it might be light-hearted: "My new religion, Tanism, only needs a great beach and the sun."

Now matter what the assignment's length is, here are some things to think about. Take any part of this that helps, but don't take any of it too seriously:

1. Do you want one god or, like the Greeks, many gods? If many, what are their names and what are their jobs?

2. Would you have a concept like sin? If not, what would take its place?

3. When would the faithful meet and how regularly? Would it be outdoors, in a church-like building, or in a condo to practice Condoism?

4. Would there be singing and reading from a text? What would the text be called? Would it be long or short, easy or hard to read?

5 Would there be an afterlife, a place like Heaven/Hell? Or would it be like summer vacation if you were good and an endless English class if you were bad?

Assignment 58

You must choose one of the following: a heartfelt and fulfilling relationship with one person but no other close friendships, or lots of dear friends but no single, enduring connection to one person. Which would you choose and why?

Comment: Unlike essay questions about the economic factors that led to World War II, there is no single right answer. If you were working with a psychologist, you might want to question the values behind the choice presented here, but you could never be wrong. You're not working with a therapist, though; you're writing for a teacher, and some of the essays will be wrong in the sense of obscure, muddled, or confusing. Like lost pioneers, they'll set off for one place and end up in another.

Learning to write for teachers is a skill like any other. If an assignment seems hard, just go back to basics. Begin, for example, by fooling with the thesis. Use some key words from the assignment. "An intimate relationship with one person would give me all the love and stability I need, so I could do without other close friends." Or, "No matter how deep and fulfilling a relationship is, I seem to get tired of it, so lots of different dear friends would be my choice."

Assignment 59

Write two letters to someone explaining a problem. Make the first letter reasonable and controlled; then write the second in a snotty and angry way.

Comment: Here is an exercise that shows <u>how</u> people write is as important as <u>what</u> they write. A breezy style might be terrific for one essay but the next one needs to be punchy and direct, the next passionate, and the next contemplative.
A simple example might be two letters to a roommate about her sloppiness. Here is reasonable and controlled:

Dear Frieda,
I know you've been busy with work and I know breaking up with Tom has you upset you . That's why I'm sure you haven't let the apartment go on purpose.

Here is snotty and angry:

Dear Frieda,
The last thing I want to see when I come home from work is your leotard in the vegetable crisper. Did you leave your brain at the gym, you moron?

One of the most disheartening things to a writing teacher is seeing the same sorts of words in the same order for every assignment. Professional writers use different writing styles for different assignments. You can, too!

Assignment 60

You are in charge of a project that will send a small unmanned capsule into deep space. The idea is to show anyone or anything that finds it what life in the U.S. is like right now. What items will you include?

Comment: This exercise could be used in a literature class during a discussion of Symbols, since the items in your space capsule will stand for life on Earth right now. Reeboks, for example, stand for the national interest in exercise and fitness just like a picture of a Big Mac symbolizes all fast food which in turn suggests the fast pace most of us live at.

It's possible to do nothing but list significant items and to write almost no exposition at all. For example, "I'd send Classic Coke, Reeboks, Levis, color picture of a Big Mac, a *New York Times*, *Newsweek* magazine, . . ."
It's an interesting idea; if it appeals to you, ask your teacher.

Most students, though, will be happier with the standard thesis. Here's a way to limit the topic and still get the job done. For a paper longer than a page you might list two or three symbols plus your reasons. "Among other things, I'd have to include a picture of a group of women, a Pro-Life pamphlet, and a Pro-Choice pamphlet to show the decisions that women are struggling with today." If you're assigned a short paper, just concentrate on one key word: "Although there's room for dozens of things, I'd be sure to send a sports page from any newspaper to show how crazy Americans are for organized sports."

Assignment 61

How many kinds of teachers are there?

Comment: A topic like this obviously it wants teachers divided up and then labeled just like the following have been divided and classified: Seven Deadly Sins, Five Ways to Succeed, Three Basic Body Types, and Four Kinds of Kisses.
I know most teachers are Good or Bad, but how about Hot and Cold teachers, Cops and Pushovers or Ins and Outs. Consider Aliens and Earthlings, or Cadillacs and Chevrolets.
What do you think of this opening?

There are two kinds of teachers who teach. Those two kinds of teachers are Inspiring Teachers and Uninspiring Teachers. Inspiring Teachers are the kind who, under most circumstances, inspire. Yes, they make us want to learn.

Not very good, is it? But a vivid and honest-sounding style, even on the same so-so topic, could be okay:

Everything about Mr. Wombat was uninspiring, from his gray hair to his gray suit to his gray, bloodless hands. He leaned against the podium like he needed a transfusion.

Assignment 62

What causes you the most emotional pain — jealousy or anger?

Comment: Take a look at two different openings for this assignment:

Jealousy is more painful to me than anger. Anger is more temporary than jealousy for me. It comes and goes, but the other stays. I can be proud of getting angry sometimes, but never of jealousy. There's never a good time for it.

Jealousy is more emotionally painful to me than anger, which is temporary. Like a fire, anger flares up and then dies. Jealousy, though, is always there, smoldering or burning out of control, but never dead.

The second is really an enhanced version of first, which hurries us through the topic like a realtor showing a house at top speed. The second lets us slow down and see the color of the carpets and the way the living room opens onto the patio.

Example number one isn't as bad as it is hasty, but in writing, like in art class, if the assignment is to bring in a painting, a pencil sketch won't do.

Assignment 63

Do you trust someone in authority if he's a sloppy dresser, has dirty fingernails, or needs a haircut? Why or why not?

Comment: Take a look at some thesis sentences, all for different-sized papers, most in different styles ranging from easy-going to angry.

1. I still trust my dad and he's always been sloppy. He's got a good heart and he's a straight-thinker.

2. I wouldn't trust anybody with power who wasn't careful about his appearance because I want someone I can look up to.

3. I don't think neat people are necessarily good workers, but I do think most good workers are neat.

4. I think neatness inspires confidence in general, so I tend to trust politicians, corporate presidents and doctors who look good.

5. Many brilliant people don't have the time or the interest to look like Sears mannequins, and criticizing them for that is just another kind of prejudice.

As usual, your teacher may ask you to make up an original thesis. If you're stumped, use the ones above as models. Play with them, change the key words, make them longer or shorter, plug in some different ideas until they're yours.

Assignment 64

During one-to-one conversations, do you listen more than you talk or vice-versa?

Comment: Take a look at these opening sentences:

1. I talk more than I listen because people come to me for advice.

2. I listen more than I talk because people come to me for advice.

Which is right? Both. Writer #1 will explain that when Bob comes to him and asks, "What can I do about Rita?" he jumps right in and gives Bob all the advice at his disposable. Writer #2, however, will explain that as Bob talks about his problem with Rita, he just listens until he knows enough to briefly advise him.

Here is another approach to this writing problem:

Whether I listen more or talk more depends on who I'm talking to and what we're talking about. I listened a lot last week when Mom talked about how much she missed Dad, but I talked more just yesterday when my son came home with a bad report card.

Here is another: "When I'm chatting with someone I talk a lot, but when we're gossiping, I listen." This student wants to write about the differences between chatting and gossiping.

Assignment 65

When you're depressed, what do you do that usually makes you feel better?

Comment: Why not just hit this one hard from the beginning: "When I'm depressed, I usually _____, and nine times out of ten I feel better."
The list of things that people do is endless: jog, lift weights, go to church, talk on the phone, pig out, write home for money, drop a class, take a class, cut a class, clean house, sleep, shop. Here's a good beginning about shopping:

When I'm depressed, nothing makes me feel better than shopping. Just wandering through the air-conditioned store helps. It's so organized, unlike my life. Then I hit Men's Sportswear, and I really start to feel good. Just look at all those cashmere socks. They'd feel terrific in Italian loafers, strolling across the carpet of my new office.

In your short essay, follow the steps to feeling better. If you jog, start the reader as you slip into your beloved Pumas. If you go to church, let everyone see and smell and feel what you do as you step through the big doors. If you pig out, we should all taste the Oreos as the French Vanilla melts in.

Assignment 66

Write a short essay about a creepy person.

Comment: Assignments like this nudge beginning writers away from some standard essay, because most people's ideas of creepiness are blessedly unique. Does creepy Tom drool on his T-shirt when he sees luscious Sheila? Or does Sheila like Tom but the other guys think he's creepy because he kisses up to the coach while everybody else is running laps in the sun? One man's creep is another man's person.
Here are some thesis sentences to prowl among:

1. I didn't think Joan was creepy until the night of Nick's party.

2. Larry isn't physically creepy, but he's got a creepy outlook on life.

3. Stan has the creepiest eyes I've even seen, and the mind to go with them.

4. Laura is a creep because she lies about everything to make herself look good.

Each of these sentences has a slightly different focus, but all of them have to be developed with vivid examples.

Assignment 67

What quality or qualities do you think a national leader should have?

Comment: Some people might say this is a hard assignment because it's so dry. I think that's true, and I also think it's hard because the essay could turn out to be so phony and pious. I can just see students dragging out poor old Abraham Lincoln. Yep, there he is now, still ruining his eyes by that famous fireplace. What are some qualities that a national leader should have? If the first things that come to mind are from the Honesty and Loyalty list, be careful. We're not talking about a Boy Scout here, but a real leader of a real nation in a real world.

Every leader needs to be intelligent, but a national leader has to be shrewd, too.

It seems to me that any national leader would have to be a quick judge of character.

I think that a national leader would have to be tough but adaptable.

No national leader can be honest about everything, or there'd be no national security, so he or she would have to know when to tell the whole truth and when to hold back.

Assignment 68

Do you think most people find statistics and incidents to prove that their point of view is the right one?

Comment: Here are some ways to look at this assignment: the person who believes that the world is a dangerous place reads the newspaper and chooses the bloodiest stories, right? Or are there really more tragic and grisly incidents than optimistic and uplifting ones? Given a lemon, do some people suck on it and complain while others make lemonade? Is the glass half-full or half-empty?

My friend, Chuck, is a good example of a guy who picks incidents to match his needs. He points out every divorced man he meets and treats the happily married ones like they're invisible.

Most of us have a big emotional investment in our beliefs, so it's natural to choose incidents that fit with who we think we are.

Being alive is like being at a buffet. We constantly choose from thousands of sights, sounds, smells, people, and things.

It's fun to theorize about stuff like this, but if guessing about other people makes for a goofy or confusing essay, ask yourself: What do I do?

Assignment 69

"Men are valued for their accomplishments while women are valued for their beauty." Is this a valid observation?

Comment: One of the first problems I see here is way the problem is presented: men are this, women are that. A clever way to begin, then, is with a phrase like, "For the most part...." or "In general...." That will soften the hard edge.

Unfortunately, the observation about the value of men and women is still valid.

In the past, women were valued for nothing except beauty, but this isn't as true today.

Beautiful women who also accomplish something are valued twice, once for their good looks and once for their success.

Women are valued for accomplishing something as long as it's centered on home or children.

Men say, "He's forty-five and worth two million." Women say, "She's forty-five and looks thirty-three." Is that valid enough for you?

Assignment 70

It's common for top female models to be paid hundreds of dollars an hour for their services. Briefly discuss why a model could be worth that much money.

Comment: A very strict teacher will not want an essay arguing that no one is worth that much money because the topic clearly asks for a discussion of why such a thing is possible.
See if these openings give you some ideas:

Designers have millions of dollars tied up in their creations. If they can find someone who makes the clothes look great, a few hundred dollars an hour doesn't seem like that much.

When an athlete can get millions for playing a game, what's so surprising about beauty being worth $400.00 an hour?

Really beautiful women are as unique as really beautiful paintings, which sell for millions. Shouldn't the real thing be worth at least a fraction of that?"

People love the ideal, so it's no wonder that models who stand for All-American Girl, Dream Mom, or Fantasy Wife get paid so much.

Assignment 71

Do highly paid athletes have more of a responsibility to their fans than those who get paid less?

Comment: *Responsibility* is the tricky word here. Does it mean responsible off the field as a role model or just on the field as a star?

Star football players are role models for thousands of kids, so they should behave themselves on and off the field.

An athlete's job is on the court, field or diamond no matter what he's paid. What he does any other time is up to him.

It's worth remembering, though, that responsibility isn't only social. Here are some openings that take another tack:

A boss gets paid more than a clerk because he has to work longer and harder. The same thing is true for a million-dollar-bonus baby.

If I pay twenty-four bucks to see a star, I want my money's worth. He owes me.

No matter how highly paid athletes are, they're not machines. An off-day shouldn't mean that a guy is irresponsible.

Assignment 72

Most everyone knows the question-and-answer columns in the newspapers: Ann Landers, Dear Abby, Miss Lonelyhearts and Help-Line are just a few. Why do you think troubled people would write to someone they had never met?

Comment: Here is a chance to review the basics: one key word in the thesis will begin a short paper or long paragraph. Add a word and meet the needs of a longer assignment. Add still another and make the essay even longer and richer.

For example, "I think that shyness might make someone write to a stranger rather than asking a friend for help." With a single key word like *shyness,* a wise student will explain his point of view and get out.
Consider, "I think loneliness and desperation might make somebody write to a stranger for advice." *Loneliness* and *desperation* are powerful words, as anybody who has been lonely and desperate knows. Discussing these two conditions vividly and wisely will take more time.

Finally, "I think troubled people write to columnists because the advice is free, they would be embarrassed to ask a friend, they believe people like Dear Abby are experts, and in some cases they don't have anywhere else to turn." With four points to bring to life, this paper will be the most complex.

Assignment 73

Evaluate the typical beauty contest. Is it just a meat market and ultimately degrading to women, or is it a harmless event that's fun to watch and could be rewarding to the contestants?

Comment: Here is an opening written by an excited student using a hot style:

The standard beauty contest is nothing but an anxiety-riddled, degrading meat market. There are the prancing prime cuts, everything from Miss Spark Plug to Miss Apprehension, parading along line wearing almost nothing but pained expressions.

This long thesis, though, is much cooler:

I admit that beauty contests can be embarrassing, but they do offer rewards ranging from new friends and increased self-esteem all the way to careers in modeling and acting.

Which style is best? Both are good; clever students choose a style that will help them write the best paper.

By the way, lots of people are against beauty contests because they often do treat women as objects. But if everyone climbs on the Bash The Contests wagon, then the single, moderate essay in favor of contests will be the unique one.

Assignment 74

What's more important to you, the things you do or the memories you have about the things you do?

Comment: This is basically a philosophical question, turning on the value of Experience vs. Memory. I wouldn't get roped into writing a philosophical essay.
In fact, this assignment should be distinguished by its down-to-earthness. Here's a sample beginning:

I loved getting married to Stan, but I almost never think back to the wedding. I'm too busy, I guess, being married right now, helping with tonight's dinner, or putting Jill to bed.

As usual, here is the other side of the coin to consider:

Doing something isn't as rewarding to me as remembering it. I'm so excitedwhen I hit a home run that it's not until later that the whole thing — the trip around the bases, the crowd yelling — is real.

Memory can be very hard to write about. But memories are a whole other thing. Open your album and show your readers the things you've done and the places you've been.

Assignment 75

In the old days, parents chose their children's husbands and wives. Why was this a good system?

Comment: The usual essay on arranged marriages says, "Wasn't-it-horrible." A clever student, though, could predict the standard outrage on most people's part and decide to be the only one in favor of arranged marriages.

Remember, this assignment asks why this was a <u>good</u> system.

Lots of people complain that today's relationships lack mystery and excitement. Well, what could be more exciting than marrying a stranger?

In the past, young people couldn't besure of ever loving their husbands or wives, but by going along with the arranged marriages they could be sure their parents were happy.

Arranged marriages were part of a good system because they avoided divorce, single-parent families, latch key kids, and hassles about alimony.

When you think about it, writing this essay is simply a necessity like some weddings in the past were necessities. At first, the young people didn't like each other any more than students like some of the essays they write. Yet some arranged marriages turned out wonderfully. And so will some of these essays.

Assignment 76

What sorts of things can happen to people to make them drastically alter the way they look at the world?

Comment: Let's begin with the obvious. A healthy woman has an accident or illness that turns her into an invalid; her optimism turns to pessimism. Though it's likely to happen this way, a reader is likely to say, "Yes, so?" Readers aren't callous people, but as readers they expect more than the obvious or if the obvious is inevitable then they expect something extra ike clever prose, charm, or special insight.
Since the obvious is always waiting in the wings and will rush out at the least sign of encouragement, let's wander around first among the other possibilities.

Is it possible that an accident or illness could have a positive effect? Sure it is. Not all accidents are tragic. I know of a successful novelist who probably wouldn't have written a word if tuberculosis hadn't forced him to drop out of medical school.

Don't forget that the assignment doesn't say that bad things have to happen. A lonely person could fall in love and have that dazzling experience alter the way he looks at the world. Someone could win the lottery and decide that life isn't so bad, after all or, with a twist, she could win it and then decide that money isn't everything.

Assignment 77

What would it take to make you give up TV?

Comment: All songs are songs, but the tunes are different. All thesis sentences are thesis sentences, but their tunes are different, too. Here are a handful to choose among. They're all on this topic, but they aren't all playing the same song.

Since I don't watch TV much, anyway, I'd give it up for a Snicker's candy bar.

It would take a girlfriend or at least a roommate to make me give up TV because I keep it on all the time just for company.

When I'm well I'd give up TV for ten dollars, but when I'm sick I wouldn't give it up for anything.

Since TV puts me to sleep every night, I'd need a lifetime supply of Doze-O sleeping pills to make me give it up.

All my friends watch TV then talk about what they saw, so to give up TV I'd need a whole new set of friends.

I couldn't live without my TV, because it's easier to understand than a book, more interesting than a husband, and cheaper than a therapist.

Assignment 78

If the opinions of others didn't matter, what might you do?

Comment: We should do what we want, regardless of what others think, and we shouldn't limit ourselves. What's wrong with being honest about our needs and desires? We should all be honest, and we shouldn't be shy and inhibited.

Besides sounding pompous and vague, this opening isn't even on the assignment, which asks what might you do, not what should you do. Lighten up a little:

If I didn't care what my parents thought, I'd move out and live with my boyfriend.

If I really didn't care what others thought, I'd get a kick out of strolling nude through the mall.

If I wasn't so conscious of other people's opinions I'd eat fudge until I weighed three hundred pounds and just say to hell with all of it.

If nobody cared what I did, I'd probably go crazy since it just occurred to me that all my values come from other people!

Assignment 79

Do most things turn out to be better or worse than they first seemed?

Comment: At the easiest level of composition, the thesis chooses one of the two key words and supports it. Here's a possible beginning:

For me, most things turn out better than they first seem. I'm the sort of person who always thinks he's made a mistake. The new car won't run, the new roof will leak or the new movie will be dull.

At another level of writing — not necessarily a better one — someone might suggest that she can influence the way things turn out.

Most things turn out better than they first seem because I want them to. If my boyfriend has to be late picking me up, I decide not to be mad. Instead, I have a Pepsi and pay some bills.

The last example has more to offer since we have some insight into how and why things turn out as they do for this writer. But the other examples are not bad or weak. They are just different. Anything that is clear and does what the assignment asks should never be criticized.

Assignment 80

You, your family, and your pets are safe, but the house is burning. A fireman can carry out one thing before the place collapses. What would you choose?

Comment: Clearly, these choices are supposed to reveal values and personalities. "Save the wedding album!" suggests a romantic person. If someone chooses the family Bible, he or she is religious. A practical person might ask for the income tax records. A writer would want an unfinished manuscript.

Start with the truth. There's a potentially rich little essay in a beginning like this one:

I'd ask the fireman for the family album because I wouldn't want to see our past go up in smoke, too. I'd hate to lose the pictures of Julie dressed up as a cloud for the kindergarten play. Or the one of Walter in his Army uniform, or of Uncle Lew showing off on the diving board at Lake Charles.

Don't panic. Jot down some things: the TV, last November's *Playboy,* the good silver, a painting, the scotch, your leather jacket, Mom's matchbook collection, or — for the Transylvanian family — the garlic.

Assignment 81

Is committing suicide a brave act or a cowardly one?

Comment: Notice, as usual, what you're being offered to work with: It seems to be the hard line: you either love me or you don't. Things are either right or they're wrong. Either/or, yes/no, black/white.

Suicide is a cowardly thing to do.Suicide is no answer to problems, even serious ones. There is always hope. It's darkest before the dawn. We should never give up but rather be brave.

My ears hurt after reading an entire essay like that. Whoever hammered it out didn't present something that readers will consider with pleasure, pleasure in the reasoning and pleasure in the writing.

Except for people whose strong religious beliefs make suicide virtually impossible, I think it might be either brave or cowardly. I'd have to know the circumstances.

This beginning lets the writer explore some possibilities. He doesn't pretend to know all the answers, but as he considers the circumstances (a broken heart, a serious illness, some agony beyond the cycle of grief as most of us know it), he'll find an answer or two, even if they're tentative.

Assignment 82

"Students who don't know the dates of America's great wars or can't draw a rough map of South America are rationally ignorant. That is, they are too smart to clutter their minds with useless information." Comment on the validity of this quotation about rational ignorance.

Comment: To help you come up with a thesis that will open an attractive essay, let's stroll through the assignment. It's asking if education is based on memory, if education is a vast collection of facts, like a button box or junk drawer, and it's asking if students are too smart to fall for such a limited definition of education. Use any of these openings that appeals to you. Or make up your own!

I don't think that knowing strange names and obscure dates is so important, but the discipline of memorizing them and being tested is. Nobody like to run laps, but nobody goes into the big race without doing them, either.

I object to the words *clutter* and *useless* in the assignment. My mind doesn't clutter like a closet; it is much more like a computer stocked with all sorts of interesting information.

Everybody I know got useless information when they were in school, and it hasn't seemed to hurt them.

Assignment 83

Assume that you've been a salesperson for a few months. You've noticed various types of customers — Gabby, Sneaky, Seductive, Helpless, Dreamy, Snotty, or Mean. Choose a type or two (or make up some of your own) and discuss in some detail.

Comment: Some essays are like flashlights; they pick out and illuminate one thing at a time. Other essays roam through the topic taking snapshots and making a history of the trip. This one develops little by little, like an artist adding detail after detail until the picture comes to life.
Pay attention to these words: " . . and discuss in some detail."

My least favorite shoppers are the mean ones. How do they get that way, so nasty and grumpy? I can hardly say, "May I help you?" before they say something mean.

This opening is not detailed enough. Are these shoppers men or women or both? What do these shoppers look like? How do they stand? What exactly do they say?

It's almost essential that you use some dialogue. "Mean people always make mean remarks," isn't nearly as potent as this. "Just yesterday a customer said, "Did you have brain damage before you started to work here?" Students shy away from dialogue, but it makes for a real sense of authenticity. Try it.

Assignment 84

All high school students should be required to take a foreign language. Agree or disagree.

Comment: The standard argument on the pro side is that learning another language is life-enhancing and culturally broadening. On the con side, foreign language programs are expensive, and language classes are hard on kids who have more pressing problems with math and English. Those are fine, and I want to suggest another angle:

I hated high school, anyway, and taking Spanish was just another pointless chore.

I got along okay in French, but I could never justify the class to my friends since it was just something I liked.

In my high school, English was the foreign language. I heard Spanish, Korean, French, and Vietnamese every day, and I learned more just listening in the cafeteria than in any class.

I went to a Catholic high school where we had to take Latin. It was hard and sometimes it was boring, but it gave me a real sense of history.

Each of the beginnings above completes the assignment by saying, in effect, "I don't know about everybody else, but my experience with languages in high school showed me this."

Assignment 85

Think back to a time when something significant happened to you, something you were directly involved with and had a big part in bringing about. If you knew then what you know now, would you have acted the same way, said the same things?

Comment: I'd begin with "something significant." This will vary from person to person, and it doesn't necessarily have to be life-threatening or shattering. Breaking up with somebody special would qualify, and so would buying a car that broke down all the time. Having a big fight with a friend seems significant; so does moving out on your own the first time. Or moving back in!

The thesis doesn't have to complicated, either, to be complete and fertile: "I wouldn't have broken up with Sarah the way I did if I'd known how hard it would be to get a new girlfriend." Isn't it curious how topics like this incline us toward the dramatic or melodramatic? "I wouldn't have gone skiing if I'd known how dangerous it was going to be." "I wouldn't have called my dad a blood-sucking, minimum wage, capitalist pig if I'd known what a dump I'd be banished to." "I wouldn't have gone into that old house after Fluffy if I'd know it was haunted."

Don't get me wrong; problems make for good dramatic writing. The worst TV show has a problem to be solved: Will Celia learn to skate? Will the ice cream melt?

Still, it might be fun to look for "something significant" that was wonderful.

Assignment 86

Think of something you're good at — playing the piano, cooking, skating, dancing or whatever. Cover the problems that a first-timer might run into.

Comment: This is an apparently simple topic, but it's like an apparently easy climb that turns perilous. The peril here is not sharp rocks or wild animals. It's the loss of your reader through boredom.

Slow dancing is easy for a guy if he follows a few simple rules. First, hold the girl firmly. Now, the easiest step is the Box Step. Feet together, left foot first — step up (not left or right), then slide right, step back, slide left. You have 'drawn' a rectangle or box.

There are, though, things to write about using slow dancing as the topic. I'd like to read an essay on holding the girl firmly and the problems an amateur might encounter. There's a certain charm, also, in a paper that begins like this:

For someone who's never eaten before, a few warnings are in order. First, that steak doesn't go down all at once. It's cut up into something called bites.

There are always topics like renting a tuxedo or borrowing money from a bank. Experiment with something livelier for your first-timer, like sleeping, kissing, buying an athletic supporter or a bra.

Assignment 87

What do you think of people who get to be rich and famous by compromising their principles?

Comment: This would be hard for me to write about because I don't know anyone who got rich or famous through compromise. I'd have to imagine someone, imagine his principles and imagine the compromising events:

When my friend Tom got rich by giving up the violin and writing popular songs instead, I felt sorry for him.

Maybe, but it sounds schmaltzy. Are wealth and fame that easy? This thesis makes it sound like Tom dropped his Stradivarius on Tuesday and by Wednesday was cranking out tunes for the Top 40. If this is true, I'm surprised the line to compromise doesn't stretch around the block.
The part of this assignment that actually interests me is the underlying assumption that compromise automatically leads to wealth and fame. The entire writing-problem is loaded down with melodrama and scenery from bad movies — the idealistic doctor who becomes a callous plastic surgeon in Beverly Hills, the honest bank clerk who wants to give farmers a fair shake and ends up foreclosing on widowed orphans.

The assignment is loaded with dangerous words. Take care.

Assignment 88

How can a teacher's effectiveness best be measured?

Comment: Let me suggest a few things for you to consider.

Is it important for a teacher to be popular? If so, what does that popularity have to do with effectiveness?

Should students regularly be given standardized tests and should teachers be evaluated by their students' scores? If so, can a standardized test in English or art measure as well as one in history or math?

Are their qualities that are hard to measure — qualities like compassion or understanding — that should be not be overlooked in any fair evaluation? If so, how can these qualities be included?

Here is a standard thesis: "An effective teacher turns out students who do well on tests." That isn't bad, but it is broad. A little whittling might get this: "Effective English teachers turn out students who can compose an essay and write clear sentences."
Here, for comparison, is a thesis with a broader base: "I think an effective teacher not only presents the material clearly but helps students to feel good about themselves, though I admit that increased self-esteem is hard to measure." It's a good thesis, but it's for a long essay. How long is your assignment today?

Assignment 89

A Peace Corps volunteer said that she was glad to be assigned to a remote village in India because she was anxious to leave behind the materialistic, acquisition-oriented U.S. for a while. What's so bad about having material things (cars, houses, boats, microwaves, etc.) and wanting more?

Comment: Most topics are like houses; there's more than one way in: front, back, sliding patio door, any window. This one is a burglar's dream — right up the walk and in the front.

What's bad about owning material things is that it's like drugs or alcohol. People always want more, more, more and that's what's wrong with this formerly great nation.

Don't you want to tell the person who wrote that to just sit down and have a glass of warm milk? As usual, it's not that he or so is wrong, but the prose is so close to hysteria that it's bound to repel more readers than it attracts.
In one sense since getting and owning are such easy targets to pick on, it might be fun to defend them.

There's nothing wrong with getting and owning things. Successful people usually live in the biggest houses and drive the shiniest cars. Since we can't look inside people to see who's happiest, we look to see who has the biggest color TV and the thickest carpet.

Assignment 90

Advertisements sometimes feature sleeping, rosy-cheeked children. Sleeping adults, though, aren't usually thought of as innocent. What do you think is lost in the process of growing up?

Comment: Using the words from the topic, the answer to the question is easy. It's innocence.

People lose their innocence as they grow up. They don't feel as pure or as naive about things. Frightening or upsetting things happen to them and their idea of the world as a warm and and cozy place is shattered forever.

Maybe, but I don't know what this writer is talking about. Does a parent get sick? Is there a divorce? Do the children get beat up at recess or criticized by a teacher? Does puberty kick in and change everything?

My parents took such took care of me that I was certain the world was a pretty dandy place until I got a terrible kidney infection when I was eight. Being in the hospital alone showed me I was mortal, and since I knew that I wasn't going to live forever I never felt exactly the same way about anything again.

Assignment 91

What do you personally do to make the world a better place?

Comment: If there's anything I like, it's a nice guilt-inducing topic. Maybe the approach is a honest one: "I don't do anything to make the world a better place, and it's none of your business, anyway."
Then again, maybe not. Here are a couple better-natured ideas for opening sentences.

I don't do anything world-shaking to make this a better place, but I do try to not get mad at people just because I'm cranky. There's enough anger around without me adding to it.

I pick up litter wherever I see it, and I hope that makes the world better. I know it's a tiny thing and my friends think I'm crazy, but I figure one less beer can or candy wrapper is bound to help.

I was talking about this topic to a class one day and a woman remarked that her contribution to the world was seven children. I thought the other students were going to string her up from the light fixture as they shouted about over-population. However, here is an angle for parents that should work:

I do my best to teach my kids to be considerate to everybody, no matter what age or race or sex.

Assignment 92

A singer who had only one Top 40 hit talked bitterly about herself as the Flavor of the Month. How tough do you think it'd be to be hot for a few weeks and then cold for a long time?

Comment: There's probably no harm in guessing how we're liable to feel about something, but I know that ways I imagine I'll feel and things I imagine I'll do don't always work out. For example, I always plan to rescue the maiden in distress and I usually end up quivering in the bushes.
The good thing about the topic is that the question ("How tough do you think it would be . . .?") can be answered directly: Very tough. Not too bad. A cinch.

It's important for me to be popular, so it'd be hard to be a TV star for a couple of months and then to slide back to normal.

I don't think it'd be too bad to feel the ups and downs of fame. Most realistic entertainers know that's the way it is. And most realistic people know that's how life is.

I think it would depend on the person. Success to immature people would mean a lot, so they'd suffer when their songs dropped off the charts. A mature singer, though, would probably just go back to the piano and the studio and keep plugging away.

Assignment 93

**More and more our experiences are programmed for us. We
hike on carefully maintained trails and look out at the ocean or
canyon from the designated spot. Do you think the view we
stumble on is more seeable than the authorized one?**

Comment: I imagine most of us think the answer to the
question is yes, because the approved view or the sanitized
wilderness experience doesn't include any surprises. Coming
around a bend and seeing a moose is a lot more exciting when
the moose hasn't been planted there by Thrilling Tours, Inc.
Here's an example of a solid opening:

I remember trudging down the Grand Canyon, dutifully
stopping with the others, dutifully following the ranger's finger
as he pointed at still another wonder. I also thought there was
something seriously wrong.
However, without maintained trails, places to pull the car safely
off the road, clean bathrooms, and handy ranger stations,
millions of people would never see any views at all. So is the
authorized version really all that bad, especially if the alternative
is staying at home and watching "Wild Kingdom" on TV?

Assignment 94

You're going to wake up in a small village located deep in the jungles of South America. The natives will be suspicious but not hostile. You will wake up knowing only four words of their language. Which four words would you like to know?

Comment: By now you recognize these assignments as the probing kind: What are your values and why? What's important to you and why? Obviously, then, someone who looks at the suspicious villagers and asks, "Where is the bar?" is different in many ways from the one who points to himself and says, "I am your king."

You can safely assume pointing and gesturing are okay, so words like *food* and *water* might be a waste of valuable vocabulary. Sort through all the things you can get or settle with mime, then experiment with really necessary words.

If you choose *God*, are you going to understand the answer? If you want an abstract word like *truth* or *justice*, what context are you going to use it in? Since I assume you're going to show up with what's in your pockets and a Bic lighter might cause quite a commotion, how about a word like *magic* ?   Would flattering words like *beautiful* or handsome help? Would you use two of your choices for *please and thanks* ?   Would you need to know *illness* or *death* ? Why? How about *happy, lonely* or afraid ?

Assignment 95

Is Truth the way things really are, or is it more like an agreement among people about how things are?

Comment: Finishing the book with a flourish, we tackle a philosophical concept. Let's begin with some prose from La-La Land:

Truth is indeed an interesting topic, one that needs discussion and deep thought. Is truth the same for all of us? Perhaps. But perhaps not. One man's truth is another's lie, isn't it?

Ninety-four other assignments have suggested direct, honest writing:

I believe Truth is the way things are. The earth is round. No matter how many people agree that it's not, any satellite picture will prove that they're wrong. And if we go out in the rain, we get wet, whether we agree to it or not.

I know that the truth can change. Once I hated my folks for being so strict with me, but I've come to understand that they meant well, and now I don't hate them anymore. Which feeling is the true one? Both.

Assignment 96

**"Success is not the answer." Briefly discuss this quote from a
well-known but disillusioned actor.**

Comment: It's true. Success isn't the answer Many rich and
famous people are successful but miserable. If success were the
answer, every successful person would be happy, but that isn't
true.

Sometimes students have trouble appreciating just how bad
writing like that is. They point out that it's grammatically
correct and that it's true, at least to the writer. Writing teachers
reply, "Sure, but it's murky and disorganized What kind of
success are we reading about? What exactly is success not the
answer to? Which famous people are miserable?

I think it's likely that a successful actor might be disillusioned
with the big salaries, fast cars, and pretty girls that usually mean
success for movies stars. Hundred dollar bills sound great to me,
but I'm a college student. If an actor is just going through the
motions making blockbuster but schlocky films, he probably
can't feel successful inside.

The second writer is less sure of himself, but he's more human!

Assignment 97

Is your individuality tolerated or encouraged?

Comment: My parents encourage my individuality. Don't get me wrong; they're not cheerleaders urging me to get into green hair. They accept me the way I am. In the last year I've been serious about yoga, vegetarianism and karate. And they still love me.

My wife tolerates my individuality, but no way does she encourage it. It's hard for her because my individuality comes out as drinkingbeer with my buddies, watching football on TV, and working on my car. She says, "Harvey, everybody does that." I reply, "Yeah, but they're all copying me.

The problem doesn't ask if individuality is criticized, but that's a possible topic, too.

I wish my individuality was at least tolerated, but the fact is that it's seriously discouraged. My boyfriend is scared of my uniqueness. When I don't dress or act like the other girls, he gets very nervous. Just last week, for example...

Assignment 98

In schools that teach Latin, this translated phrase is prominent in some classrooms: Do What You're Doing. Without limiting your discussion to school, what do you think it means?

Comment: I don't think the phrase Do What You're Doing means anything. It's just nonsense. Who can do two things at once, for heaven's sake. I can't fix my car and mow the lawn, too, can I?

The problem with this opening isn't that the writer is angry, though the essay probably whines a little too much. The real problem is that the prose isn't thoughtful. Most of us <u>can </u>do two things at once — fix dinner and think about a friend, change the spark plugs and listen to the ball game. As writers, it's not wise to overlook the obvious. Here is an opening that is more successful:

I believe Do What You're Doing means to concentrate, to not be distracted. It's good advice but easier said than done. My mind darts all over the place like a hungry bird. I'm typing while I'm planning next week's dinner; then I think of the beach which reminds me of swimming which reminds me I'm getting fat.

Assignment 99

Cultural anthropologists claim that for the first time in history, the old are learning from the young. What do you think they're learning?

Comment: Here is a buffet of openings. One of these should appeal to almost everyone. If not, whip one up from scratch.

Though the 60's were too touchy-feely for some people, I think the old could have learned from their grandchildren to be more out-going and demonstrative.

I think the young are teaching older people to be scared. Anybody born after atomic weapons were invented knows he's not exactly safe.

Young people don't conform like they used to. Sure, we dress like our friends and use the same slang, but underneath we're individuals. Older people are unique, too; I'll bet they learned that from us.

I think we're teaching older people to be idealistic again.

Old folks are learning how to be selfishfrom their nieces and nephews. All kids think about is me, me, me and now the grandparents are doing it, too.

Assignment 100

If you could reclaim an item, attitude, or feeling from your childhood, what would it be?

Comment: I'd like to have my childhood sense of freedom back. Being grown-up has cramped my style a lot. I'm too inhibited to jump up and down in puddles. I can't just plop down in the aisles at Sears and cry like I used to.

I wish I had my Speedo red wagon back. What a beauty it was. I could sit in that wagon and pretend I was driving a race car, a covered wagon, or a space ship.

Not all children are as optimistic as I once was because they have painful and confusing childhoods. But until I was ten, things went well for me. Optimism was a pleasant habit.

All of the above are, in their own ways and different styles, promising openings. They feel honest and real; they're not sentimental or blustery; they're direct, to the point, and simple in an eloquent way. Unfortunately, most students have been reared on textbook writing which is often formal and dry; most texts are, frankly, dreadful models for new writers. So don't write textbooks, okay? Write from the heart.